dressed for the occasion

BRANDON MARIE MILLER

LERNER PUBLICATIONS COMPANY • MINNEAPOLIS

For Stacy Schlenker Chael, extraordinary sister!
And with my appreciation to editor Sara Saetre

Website address: www.lernerbooks.com

Library of Congress Cataloging-in-Publication Data

Miller, Brandon Marie.
        Dressed for the occasion : what Americans wore 1620–1970 / by
Brandon Marie Miller.
            p.   cm.
        Includes bibliographical references and index.
        Summary: Examines the history, manufacture, and care of American
clothing from colonial times to the 1970s and discusses its
relationship to the social milieu.
        ISBN 0-8225-1738-8 (alk. paper)
        1. Costume—United States—History—Juvenile literature.
2. Fashion—United States—History—Juvenile literature.
[1. Costume—History. 2. Fashion—History.] I. Title.
GT605.M55   1999
391'.00973—dc21   98-22668

Manufactured in the United States of America
1 2 3 4 5 6 – JR – 04 03 02 01 00 99

Contents

"THE ART OF DRESS"

*Why should our garments, made
  to hide
Our parents' shame, provoke
  our pride?
The art of dress did ne'er begin
Till Eve, our mother, learned
  to sin.*
—Divine Songs for Children,
  1600s

'Tis sunrise on a July morning at Plymouth, Massachusetts, 1627. Mistress Bridget Fuller rises with the sun and straightens her night-gown, a knee-length shift that now becomes her undergarment for day. Over it she dons a stiffened corset, lacing it about her torso, then pulls on several long woolen skirts called petticoats. To protect her outer petticoat, she ties on a long apron. She slips into a short, fitted jacket—her waistcoat. Then, because women modestly cover their heads, she bundles her hair into a linen coif, or cap. This she will wear all day, indoors and out.

Master Samuel Fuller climbs out of bed wearing a linen shirt. He tightens the drawstring on the neck of the shirt, then covers the shirt with a short jacket called a doublet. He tugs on baggy knee-length breeches and long woolen stockings called hose, anchoring the hose to his breeches with strings called points. Last, he too dons a cap.

The Fullers' toddler son wears a long, loose dress, for boys do not wear breeches until age four or five. Learning to walk is difficult in a long, tripping gown, so the boy's head is protected from bruising by a padded "pudding cap." On his sleeve is sewn a cord called a lead string, which his busy mother uses to keep him close at hand. The older children in the Fuller family dress in adult styles, copy adult manners, and help with adult work.

Mistress Fuller knits her family's hose and sews their shifts and shirts, aprons and caps. She lacks the skill, however, to fit other garments properly. The few waistcoats, doublets, and breeches the Fullers own are clothes they brought with them from England when they journeyed to America, several years before.

TRANSPLANTS IN A NEW WORLD

In the early 1600s, European investment companies actively recruited people willing to uproot for the wilds of America. Colonists could send fur, timber, and, most hopefully, gold back to them from the New World. Some companies, including the Virginia Company and the Massachusetts Bay Company, offered doublets, breeches, stockings, and shoes as incentives to journey across the Atlantic.

People like the Fullers became colonists for religious reasons. Known as Separatists, and later called Pilgrims, they had separated from the Church of England, which they viewed as corrupt. Another group of colonists, the Puritans, also fled the "impure" Church of England. The plain dress favored by both the Pilgrims and the Puritans in New England reflected their disapproval of the English monarchy and high church.

In Virginia, Maryland, and the Carolinas, most colonists had come to the New World seeking land, wealth, and a better life. Wealthy landowners clung to aristocratic English customs. To display their status, they ordered dressy clothes and bolts of rich fabrics from London. They hired servants to help them dress and care for their wardrobes. America might be newly settled, but rich colonists' clothes must show they were not peasants.

Most colonists owned few garments, however. All clothing had value in the colonies. Unmarried men were taxed according to the worth of their wardrobes. Connecticut taxed fabric costing more than three shillings per yard. Even poor clothing was worth stealing. "I have nothing at all...no Clothes, but one poor suite, nor but one paire of shooes," reported an indentured servant in 1623. "My Cloke [cloak] is stolen by one of my own fellowes. . . . Some of my fellows saw him have butter and beef out of a ship, which my Cloke . . . paid for, so that I have not a penny."

NATIVE AMERICANS

As the first Europeans encountered Native Americans along the Atlantic coast, they labeled the Indians "barbarous and naked people." Unlike European men, who covered themselves in pounds of heavy woolen clothing, native men often wore only a loin cloth. Native women dressed in knee-length skirts. Indian children ran naked through their villages. Moccasins made of animal hide and sandals woven from plant fibers protected Indian feet. For winter warmth, people bundled up in thick fur robes made from otter, beaver, and bear skins. Native Americans decorated their clothing with fringe, shells, and stones. Some native clothing was adorned with pearls.

Anytime a hunter killed a deer for food, he supplied his family with the deer hide for clothes. Native American women scraped the hide clean of tissue and hair, soaked it in chemicals (usually water mixed with bark from oak and hemlock trees), then dried the skin, greased it with fats, and softened it into a buttery smooth fabric by hand rubbing. Finally, they sewed the tanned buckskin into garments. White colonists, especially families on the frontier, also made buckskin clothes.

Colonists in high-crowned hats bartered for a deer hide with native men clothed in buckskin.

Native Americans also traded furs to European trappers. Soft, thick beaver fur was especially prized; fur trappers couldn't send enough beaver pelts to Europe. There, the undercoat of a beaver pelt was pressed and steamed into a luxurious, velvety felt and made into high-crowned hats. But many tribes paid dearly for the trade in furs. Trappers brought deadly foreign diseases with them as they traveled their trading routes. Some tribes, such as the Hurons, lost nearly half their members by mid century.

FASHION BASICS

Clothing, like a badge, reflected a person's status in colonial society. A man was judged by the quality of his hat. A high-crowned hat, made of black beaver felt and often decorated with plumes or ribbon

In 1645, a Puritan woman made a fashion statement with a man-styled hat over a linen coif, a fancy petticoat, and a collar edged with lace. Her stepson wore a doublet and baggy breeches.

bands, marked him as a gentleman. So did a fine, clean linen shirt showing at his coat collar and cuffs. A favorite frill for both men and women was slashing a coat sleeve, allowing the shirt beneath to peep through.

For years the standing ruff, made popular by the Dutch, was the fashion rage for both men and women. Starched stiff, folded, pressed, or even wired, a ruff seemed to serve the wearer's head upon a ruff platter. By the 1630s, the standing ruff drooped to a "playne band," a large, crisply starched linen collar that fell over the shoulders.

Throughout the 1600s, women continued wearing many petticoats. A woman's top petticoat was sometimes split open in the front, or she wore it looped up, to display a fancier skirt underneath. Some women supported their heavy petticoats with a narrow hoop frame, tied about the waist. Women also wore man-styled hats, usually over their linen caps. Sometimes they draped their heads in scarflike hoods, the finest made of silk.

Colonists favored rich colors: blue, red, green, black, orange, and yellow. They relied on plant leaves, roots, and juices to dye their cloth. Indigo transformed fabric to favorite shades of blue. Madder stained cloth red; sassafras turned it orange or yellow.

"INTOLERABLE PRIDE IN CLOTHES"

As the earliest days of hardship slipped away, more colonists began purchasing fabrics and trims from England. Even in Puritan Massachusetts a bit of finery was permissible for the social elite. After all, Puritans believed a man's success reflected God's approval.

But too much indulgence in finery might also display the sin of pride. Puritan ministers preached against rich fashion. "Why should our garments, made to hide our parents' shame, provoke our pride?" wrote one reverend. In Pennsylvania, Quakers tried to live by William Penn's advice that fashion be "simple and plain. . . . Neither unshapely, or fantastical and for use and decency, not for Pride."

Early Plymouth colonist Miles Standish in a standing ruff

In some colonies, rich fashions were illegal for ordinary folk. Several colonies passed sumptuary laws, long known in Europe, to "suppress excess in cloaths." People who dressed in finery above their "place" got presented at court and fined. In 1621, Virginia decreed that only government officials could wear gold on their clothes. In Massachusetts in 1634, only a narrow edging of lace on linen was allowed. Clothes with too much lace or embroidery, or embellished with gold or silver thread, could be confiscated. In 1651, a Massachusetts court noted its "utter detestation" that men with little money or education "should take upon them the garbe of gentlemen by wearinge of gold or silver lace, or buttons." That court was equally dismayed to see "women of the same ranke . . . wear silke or hoods or scarfs." A few years later, Puritan officials banned "immoderate great breeches," double ruffles, and silk roses on shoes.

In all the colonies, sumptuary laws proved difficult to enforce. Gradually, such laws gave way to people's desire for a bit of high fashion. Colonists with money soon dressed their families as well as gentlemen in England dressed theirs.

"BUSHES OF VANITY"

Although breeches remained the fashion for men throughout the 1600s, the fashion for "immoderate great breeches" waned. Breeches grew less baggy as time passed. By 1660, men wore a long vest known as a waistcoat. As an outer garment, the waist-length doublet gave way to a knee-length coat.

Around 1675, men of stature began to adopt a new fashion from France—wigs. They cut their own hair short or even shaved it off to make room for the new look. The most elaborate hairpieces were "full-bottomed" wigs with curls that fell below the shoulders. Made of human hair, horse hair, goat hair, and even silk thread, wigs were expensive. Men took to carrying their hats for fear of squashing their valuable finery. Hairpieces were often stolen by "wig snatchers," who yanked them off heads in busy city streets and darted away, leaving the

The full-bottomed wig, sweeping hat, and ruffles of this English colonial governor were fashions only the privileged enjoyed.

victims with nothing but their unfashionable shaved heads showing.

Many Puritan ministers preached against the fanciest wigs, calling them "bushes of vanity." They compared wig wearers to "locusts that come out of the bottomless pit." Other ministers, however, wore wigs themselves, including religious leader Cotton Mather. Mather even preached against the "wig haters."

AN AVERSION TO SOAP AND WATER

The smells of daily life—sweat, animal odors, and fireplace smoke—clung to people and their clothes in colonial America. People ate most foods with their fingers, and their clothes displayed many a greasy spot from wiped hands. Even so, most clothes were rarely washed. Women spot-cleaned some garments with vinegar or white wine, then stored them in chests, layering them with pine needles or cloves in an effort to keep them smelling sweet—a losing battle! And nothing could stop fleas, lice, and bedbugs from burrowing into un-washed clothes.

Only clothes made of linen—aprons, caps, and underclothes (shirts and shifts)—were laundered regularly, once every six weeks or so. Doing laundry was a time-consuming, harsh job. People had to lug buckets of water from a well or stream, then slowly heat it over a fire. After boiling the dirty clothes, colonists scrubbed them clean with a primitive soap made of animal fat, wood ash, and lye.

The bodies beneath the grimy clothes were often grimy as well. Queen Elizabeth I, who died in 1603, amazed her subjects by bathing "once a month, whether she needed to or not." Carrying and heating water for bathing was thought wasteful work. Bathing was also thought unhealthy. In winter, most homes were freezing cold away from the fireside. Removing warm clothes to climb into a tub of water just invited chills and ills to seep into the body. To mask their stench, people perfumed themselves liberally. They wore under-clothes not to protect their skin from scratchy outer clothing, but to protect the clothes from the filthy bodies underneath.

HOMESPUN LINEN AND WOOL

In most colonial families, women made fabric at home. The flax plant, used to make linen, was grown by most colonists owning a patch of land. Ripened flax had to be soaked and dried several times, then pounded with a heavy flax brake. The fiber was then spun into thread on a spinning wheel, woven into cloth on a loom, and "whitened" with buttermilk or a mixture of water and ashes. Finally, over long winter nights, mothers, daughters, and sons stitched linen into clothing. From flax plant to finished linen shirt required about a year of labor.

Like linen, wool called for months of work. In spring, a family sheared its sheep, then washed and fluffed the wool. Next they carded, combed, and spun it into yarns and threads. An accomplished spinner produced six skeins of yarn in one day. One durable, if itchy, fabric of early America, linsey-woolsey, was made by weaving threads of wool and linen together.

Sewing and knitting skills, as well as skills in preparing cloth, were taught to every daughter and to many sons. Most women continually sewed and mended. Clothes were handed down or remade until finally the cloth became scraps for quilts and rags. Buttons (made of pewter, bone, or wood) were snipped from worn-out garments and used again.

Most of the colonies promoted cloth production. Sheep were allowed to graze on shared land in villages. Massachusetts encouraged unemployed persons—single women, girls, and boys—to spin by awarding prizes for the finest spinning. The Virginia Assembly decided 5 children could weave enough cloth to dress 30 people and planned to set up schools to teach weaving to children.

Exporting woolen goods, however, was another matter. England expected the colonies to support English industry by supplying raw materials and buying finished English goods. Beginning in 1651, England passed a series of laws to regulate colonial trade. One was the Wool Act of 1699, which prohibited the export of woolen goods. Many colonists resented these laws, which "draw all the wealth" of the colonies "into [England's] own stock." Of course, from the English point of view, that was the purpose of the colonies.

FASHIONS OF INDEPENDENCE

To be out of fashion is more criminal than to be seen in a state of nature.
—Abigail Adams, writing from Paris, September 1784

To be seen at Mrs. Hannah Teatt's," read the dressmaker's advertisement in the *New England Weekly Journal* in 1733, "... a baby dressed after the newest fashion ... from London." People greeted Mrs. Teatt's announcement with excitement. The baby was a jointed fashion doll on display in her shop. It took four or five months for fashion dolls to arrive from Europe, wearing the latest styles.

The glittering court of the French kings dominated fashion in the 1700s. Americans, however, usually adopted less extreme versions of the fussy, huge European styles. How others regarded you depended upon how fashionably you dressed. Choices in fabric, trims, and styles were carefully considered.

For women with money, dresses of rich fabrics such as silk, taffeta, and brocade sported a wealth of lace, bows, and ruffles sweeping the tops of high-heeled shoes. Dress tops, called bodices, fit snugly. Necklines swooped low and squarish, though modest women covered up with a delicate fichu, worn draped over the chest like a scarf. Women continued looping up or splitting open their overskirts to reveal fancy petticoats underneath. By wearing different petticoats with a gown, a woman gave it a whole new look.

The girls, **above,** *wore panniers under their elegant gowns. All these children wore corsets.*

"TO DIVERT THE LADIES"

Beginning in the 1730s, well-dressed women wore support hoops, called panniers, that stretched into an oval frame extending over the hips. Made of whalebone or cane, panniers shaped a gown flat in front and back, but protruded to the sides; women could rest their elbows on their skirts. A woman hung a small bag called a pocket beneath her skirts, which she reached through a slit in her gown.

Panniers created the illusion of a small waist—a fashion ideal. But the main agent of waist perfection was the corset. Cone-shaped and lined with bone, corsets encased a woman from armpits to hips. Corsets also held a woman's posture in the correct position. Even a woman clothed in plain woolen petticoats wouldn't have dreamed of dressing without a corset.

As in the previous century, children continued dressing as miniature adults. Parents obsessed about their children's posture, and both boys and girls wore corsets to straighten their spines. Some parents even strapped their children to chair backs for short periods of time.

While lovely to look at, clothing for women and girls in the 1700s was weighty and constricting. One observer, Doctor Benjamin Rush, blamed men. "I . . . ascribe the invention of ridiculous and expensive fashions in female dress entirely to the gentlemen," he wrote in 1787, ". . . to divert the ladies from improving their minds . . . and to secure more arbitrary and unlimited authority over them." English feminist Mary Wollstonecraft agreed. "An air of fashion," she claimed, "is but a badge of slavery."

This cartoon ridiculed two extremes: tight corsets and towering hairdos.

The Maryland gentleman, right, wore slim knee breeches and a richly embellished coat and waistcoat. He carried a tricorn hat.

GENTLEMEN'S DRESS

American men in the 1700s did not shy away from vivid colors and embroidered coats. John Hancock, a signer of the Declaration of Independence, was described as wearing a bright blue coat over a white satin waistcoat, white silk stockings, red shoes, and a red cap.

On well-dressed men, ruffles drooped from large coat cuffs and cascaded beneath the chin. Slim knee breeches fit over long stockings held up with garters. Square-toed leather shoes sported silver buckles. The sweeping men's hats of the late 1600s gave way to a smaller version with the brim fastened up on the sides, making the new style a three-cornered, or tricorn, hat.

Early in the 1700s, wigs began to adorn the heads not only of gentlemen, but also those of servants, military men, and tradesmen. A man could choose from many styles: a bobbed short wig, a set of rolled curls over the ears, or a ponytail tied back with a ribbon. Wigs were powdered white with flour or starch. Oil applied first helped the powder stick.

FANS AND MORE POWDER

Besides kidskin gloves and a fine lace handkerchief, one of an 18th-century woman's most important accessories was a fan. Fans were fashioned from gauze, silk, paper, feathers, and laces. A fan could conceal or reveal. If a woman drew her fan across her cheek, she was signaling to a man that she loved him. Twirling her fan in her right hand informed him that she loved someone else. To better spy on fellow guests at parties, some women carried fans wearing painted faces with the eyes cut out. "Aid-to-memory" fans listed dance steps, words to songs, and game rules for the forgetful.

By 1750, men set aside their wigs. Both men and women began to have their own hair oiled and powdered. People covered their clothes with a powdering jacket and hid their faces in a paper cone as a servant poofed nearly a pound of flour over their heads with a bellows. In grand houses, a special room was set aside for this process—the powder room. Oiled and floured hair did not improve the cleanliness of 18th-century citizens.

"RASCALLY AMERICANS"

By the early 1700s, hat making had begun to thrive in America. Britain responded with the Hat Act of 1732, which forbade the export of beaver felt hats made in the colonies. Britain forced Americans to buy British-made goods and pay heavy taxes on them. Consequently, Americans paid four times more for cloth and clothing than people in Great Britain, adding to the grievances leading to the American Revolution (1776–1783). "A colonist cannot make a button," declared the *Boston Gazette* in 1765, " . . . but some . . . respectable buttonmaker of Britain shall bawl and squall that his

This man followed the upper-class style of powdered hair. The rolled curls over his ears may have been false.

honor . . . is most . . . maltreated, injured, cheated, and robbed by the rascally Americans."

During the Revolution, Britain stopped trade with the rebellious colonies and interrupted the flow of goods from other nations into America. As goods grew scarce, Abigail Adams wrote to her husband John in France, where he served as a diplomat. She begged him to send fabrics, silk gloves, laces, and pins. "A little of what you call frippery," she reminded him, "is very necessary towards looking like the rest of the world."

For most of the war years, American soldiers faced the same short-ages as civilians. While the British army marched in matching red coats, the Continentals fought in clothes they'd worn from home. Congress could not afford to replace soldiers' clothing, and many men wore their clothes until they turned to rags. So grave was the lack of decent shoes that when the Continental army trudged to its winter quarters in 1777, George Washington mourned, "You might have tracked the army from White Marsh to Valley Forge by the blood of their feet."

In 1778 a shipment of brown and blue uniform coats arrived from France, America's ally in the fight against Great Britain. For the first time, a large segment of the American army dressed alike. But the Continentals never matched the colorful, well-dressed British and French troops. At Yorktown in 1781, British general Lord Charles Cornwallis felt too disgraced to surrender to an army of ragged colonials. Instead he pleaded sick and sent a junior officer to present the sword of surrender.

After the war, Washington made a political statement with his inaugural attire. Known for his fine clothes, he pledged his 1789 presidential oath in a dark brown suit cut from fabric made in America.

THE FRENCH REVOLUTION

In France during the 1770s, Queen Marie Antoinette and her ladies carried fashions to ridiculous extremes. Their most lavish gowns, supported by panniers, extended over five feet across—a width few doorways in America could accommodate. Their hairdos towered a foot and a half high, balancing masses of wire frame, pads, and false hair. Ribbons, plumes, miniature ships, even caged birds adorned the mounds of hair. And if the head of a great lady itched? She carried a special wand to reach inside the hairdo and scratch.

The French Revolution (1789–1795) swept away the power of the French royalty and the fashions linked with them. Interest turned to the days of the ancient Roman Empire, when people wore clothes that draped softly over the body's natural shape. A new "empire" style for women emerged: a slender, high-waisted gown with short, puffed

George Washington and his reception guests wore their hair powdered.
Martha Washington carried an important accessory—a fan.

sleeves, often made of thin muslin. In chilly weather, the thin gowns were freezing to wear, and gowns made of velvet with high necks and long sleeves soon became part of the look.

Since no corsets, heavy petticoats, or hoops were required, the weight women carried around in clothing dropped by many pounds. Simpler hairstyles supplanted powdered hair. Flat-heeled shoes replaced high heels. Fashions allowed women greater physical freedom than women had known for centuries.

A change in children's attire was also in the air. French philosopher Jean Jacques Rousseau argued against the custom of strapping young-sters into corsets:

> The limbs of the growing child should be free to move easily....The best plan is to keep children in frocks [loose

Empire gowns were often made of muslin or other cotton fabrics.

A small boy of the late 18th century

dresses] for as long as possible. . . . Their defects of body and mind may all be traced to the same source, the desire to make men [or women] of them before their time.

Children's corsets soon vanished. Simple dresses made of soft muslin, with a sash at the waist, appeared for girls and small boys. Older boys dressed for the first time in pantaloons, a version of long trousers, that buttoned onto short jackets. Artists revealed the era's new informality by depicting children with merry eyes, hugging a parent or climbing onto a parent's lap.

"KING COTTON"

By the late 1700s, machinery performed some of the work involved in making cloth. The "spinning jenny" (1765), "flying shuttle" (1773), and steam-powered loom (1785) increased the speed and quantity of fabric production, especially in Great Britain. The new craze was for fabrics such as calico, chintz, and muslin, made from

A textile mill in 1820

cotton grown in India, another colonial possession of Great Britain. Cottons took well to improved methods for dying fabrics in bright colors and patterns.

Soon America's own cotton industry was flourishing. "The four southernmost States make a great deal of cotton," noted Thomas Jefferson in a 1786 letter. "Their poor are almost entirely clothed with it. . . and even [the richer class] wear a great deal of homespun cotton." In 1793, American Eli Whitney invented the cotton gin, and cotton production soared. The cotton gin cleaned more cotton in one day than a person could clean by hand in a year.

New textile mills in New England, as well as the mills in Great Britain, clamored for raw cotton to turn into cloth. Before long, many young New England women worked in mills. The girls lived in supervised boarding houses that provided libraries and improvement societies; their jobs gave them the chance to earn independence as well as a wage. About 12,000 people worked in the mills around 1820. By the 1830s, that number climbed to 55,000.

Soon millions of acres in the South were planted in cotton. "King Cotton" ruled the southern economy. As more land was planted in cotton, more and more slaves were bound over to pick it. As many as two million slaves toiled in America's cotton fields by the 1850s.

Slaves carrying cotton in baskets

Slaves who worked in their owners' houses had better clothing than field hands; they might even dress in hand-me-down clothes from the white family. The "maids dress" at one South Carolina plantation included "linsey-woolsey gowns and white aprons in the winter, and in summer...blue homespun." A less fortunate former slave described his scant wardrobe: "No shoes, no stockings, no jacket, no trousers; nothing but coarse sack-cloth or tow-linen, made into a sort of shirt, reaching down to my knees. This I wore night and day, changing it once a week."

"TASTE AND INGENUITY"

Taste and ingenuity, with a very small amount of cash, will enable a lady to appear always fashionably attired.
—Godey's Lady's Book,
September 1845

The less a gentleman is noticeable, the more he is elegant," claimed Englishman George "Beau" Brummel in 1815. A fashion leader, Brummel was heralding a significant shift in male attire. Bright colors faded from men's fashion in the 1800s, not to return for over a century. Instead, male elegance now equaled well-tailored clothes in muted colors: A gentleman wore gray, black, and tan, and dark blues and greens.

Elegant clothes should also be clean, Brummel decreed: polished boots (Brummel rubbed his with champagne) and sharply starched collars set off with a snowy cravat. For the first time, elegance also meant personal cleanliness. Brummel bathed regularly in 15 quarts of water and 2 quarts of milk.

Brummel first popularized for men the long pantaloons that boys wore, and knee breeches retired. Pantaloons fit smooth and tight; they were kept from riding up by a strap under the foot. Made of light colors, pantaloons contrasted with coats and waistcoats.

Meanwhile, men's long waistcoats had shrunk to the waistline. So had the front of the outer coat, though the tails still hung to the knees in back. To achieve an eye-catching masculine shape, men strapped on corsets and padded their chests and shoulders. A new hat style, the top hat, appeared.

The slim, high-waisted fashion in women's dress did not last long. Bit by bit, waistlines lowered to the natural waist, and corsets reappeared. By the 1830s, "wide" was the word. Beneath their tiny waists, women wore flaring skirts shortened to the ankle. Heavy petticoats returned. Huge leg-of-mutton sleeves ballooned from dropped shoulders and horizontal necklines. To accessorize, women chose bonnets made of straw and trimmed with ribbon. Huge shawls were the rage.

"PROGRESS OF FEMALE IMPROVEMENT"

In 1830 publisher Louis Godey founded a new magazine for women called *Godey's Lady's Book.* Readership took off in 1837 when widow Sarah Josepha Hale became editor, a post she held until age 90 in 1877. The magazine offered the latest fashion news, complete with illustrations.

Godey's usually modified French fashion for American tastes and wallets. Women picked the fashion ideas that worked for them: a change in dress trim, the new full sleeves, the latest in bonnet ribbons. "Pay attention to . . . costume," Mrs. Hale advised readers, "and . . . conform to the prevailing modes of dress."

For thousands of women, *Godey's* provided the last word not only on dress, but also on womanhood. People believed women exerted a strong moral influence over their families and society. A woman's

Opposite, *bonnets and top hats were fashionable in the 1830s.*

outward appearance reflected her inner modesty and decency. The more feminine and attractive a woman, the better her ability to influence society. "Character is displayed, yes! moral taste and goodness, or their perversion, are indicated in dress," declared *Godey's* in 1837.

SUFFERING FOR FASHION

Although considered fragile by society, women daily bore a burden of garments weighing from 15 to 20 pounds. Beneath her daytime dress a woman wore at least two layers of thick petticoats to hide the scandalous shape of her legs. Evening dress required up to six petticoats. "We can expect but small achievement from women," sighed one female magazine writer, "so long as it is the labor of their lives to carry about their clothing."

Women laced their corsets more tightly than ever. A waist span under 20 inches was the goal; teenagers tried to match their waist sizes to their ages. Tight lacing squeezed a woman's ribs and pushed her internal organs out of place. Physical exercise, even sitting or walking, was difficult; bending over was nearly impossible. Working women wanted the proper silhouette, but they had to be able to move. They did wear corsets, but not laced to the point where movement was impossible.

Through the 1840s and 1850s, skirts continued to sweep fuller. By mid century, a woman had so much fabric bunched around the waist that her bodice had to be lined with bone to keep its shape smooth. More petticoats! came the cry, but, oh, the bulk and weight! A new undergarment came to the rescue—the crinoline, a petticoat stiffened with horsehair. One crinoline could hold a dress out as well as several old-fashioned petticoats.

Within a few years, the crinoline was outdone by another innovation, a huge cage made of thin steel hoops. Since dresses swung like bells over the hoop, women could move their legs more freely than when swishing through layers of petticoats. But women wearing hoops could not easily fit into spaces designed for normal humans.

They mashed together in carriages and stepped too close to fireplaces, catching their gowns on fire. "Every woman today is a tempest," noted one journalist. "She cannot enter or leave a room without knocking over everything in her path." The New York Omnibus Company raised fares from 7¢ to 12¢ for "ladies wearing hoops."

A woman in hoops also faced embarrassment if a windy gust blew beneath her cage. As a precaution, some women adopted underwear, or "drawers," such as men wore. A woman in hoops could not easily pull down her drawers to go to the bathroom, so women's drawers were crotchless. Eventually women's drawers took on their own feminine name, "pantalets."

The sweeping gowns of mid century turned women into tempests.

Pantalets saved girls in hoops from embarrassment.

Older girls also surrendered the freedom of loose dresses for hoops and tight corsets. As a nod toward more active clothing, girls wore pinafores—aprons that hung from the shoulders—to protect their clothes. People could judge a girl's age by the length of her skirt. Small girls wore loose, calf-length dresses. After age 8, a girl wore her hems just below the knee. By 16, a young lady wore long gowns like a woman.

"PROPERLY" ATTIRED

Women of money—and fashion—in the 1800s attended many different social events throughout the day, all requiring different costumes. They often changed clothes six or seven times between morning and night. Around the house a morning gown allowed for loosened corsets. Tailored suits were proper attire for walking. Evening gowns with bare arms came out on gala occasions.

After the invention of photography in the 1840s, the stately, prosperous look of politicians and businessmen spread quickly as the fashion ideal for men. Businessmen wore the sober suit of mid century: the dignified frock coat with vest and trousers. Most businessmen wore shoes and boots of black leather.

A man's shirt still distinguished his position in society. A gentleman seldom wore a shirt, considered an undergarment, without wearing a coat over it. Shirtsleeves were for manual labor such as farming. A southern woman described how one family generation would make money by toiling in shirtsleeves; then the next generation would spend it, leaving the third generation to toil in shirtsleeves again. There were seldom more than three generations, she declared, "between shirt sleeves."

Throughout the last half of the 1800s, men sprouted bushy sideburns, walrus mustaches, and beards. During the 1860 presidential race, 11-year-old Grace Bedell wrote presidential candidate Abraham

Promenade, or walking, attire, left, *and evening dress,* right. *The frock coat,* left, *became popular by 1850. The earlier style, tails and pantaloons,* right, *still served as evening wear.*

This elegant silk hoop dress was unmistakably upper class.

Lincoln to tell him he'd look better with a beard. The two met as Lincoln traveled to his inauguration. "You see," the bearded president-elect told her, "I have let these whiskers grow for you, Grace."

MOURNING

When a 19th-century woman's husband died, society insisted her behavior reflect her grief. She withdrew from all social outings. For at least the first year after a husband's death, a widow could not think of remarriage; people believed it took that long for the dead man's body to rot in the grave.

A widow's clothes also demonstrated her rejection of joy. For the first year, she wore "deepest mourning": Everything from gowns to gloves must be black. She limited her jewelry to mourning rings or brooches made from the deceased's hair. Women who could not afford new dresses of the proper dull black crepe dyed their old dresses black.

During the second year of mourning, a widow's social circle widened. A bit of black decoration or jewelry relieved her severe dresses. After two and a half years, "half-mourning" colors such as violet, gray, and white were permitted. Mourning clothes worn for different occasions all had to be an appropriate mourning color.

And what did society expect of a husband if his wife died? He wore black clothes and a black armband for several months.

Mourning stores such as the Family Mourning Store of Boston catered to the needs of the bereaved, carrying black cloth ("Superior English Crepe") and mourning clothes and accessories. Mourning stores encouraged the idea that once official mourning ended, storing crepe in the house was unlucky. If a woman needed mourning clothes again, she'd have to buy new.

"GOODS SUITABLE FOR THE MILLIONAIRE"

*The more work can be done . . .
by means of machines—the
greater will be the demand. Men
and women will disdain . . .
a nice worn garment, and
gradually we shall become a
nation without spot or blemish.*
— New York Tribune,
late 1850s

"The bridesmaids were dressed in black," noted a guest at a South Carolina wedding in 1864, "the bride in Confederate gray homespun. She had worn the dress all winter, but it had been washed and turned for the wedding. The female critics pronounced it 'flabby-dabby.' They also said her collar was only 'net,' not lace. . . . Her bonnet was homemade."

During the American Civil War (1861–1865), clothing and fabric shortages affected all Americans, but especially those in the South. The North's effective naval blockade prevented ships from carrying goods into Southern ports, causing shortages in clothing, blankets, and bandages. Yet early on, "fashions from France still creep into Texas across the Mexican border," wrote a Southern woman in 1861.

Prices for everything soon soared. When one woman's mother-in-law died, the younger woman paid $500 for a mourning dress, veil, bonnet, and gloves. Even at that price the quality was so poor she declared, "Before the blockade, these things would not have been thought fit for a chambermaid!"

Above, *women who followed their husbands to war found laundry and mending to be endless tasks.* **Opposite,** *Tad Lincoln was President Abraham Lincoln's son.*

As the war dragged on, cotton production virtually halted. Families dragged spinning wheels and looms out of storage and produced simple homespun clothes, sometimes with fabric woven from cotton mattress stuffing. They knitted socks from unraveled wool blankets and made shoes from leather hats. In a patriotic fervor, women ripped up silk gowns for battle flags. They sold their finery to buy necessary goods, especially food. "What a scene!" described one upper-class seller. "Such piles of rubbish, and mixed up with it such splendid Paris silks and satins."

Without Southern cotton, some textile mills in Northern states closed. Northern women began to economize on dress, turning old gowns inside out to use the protected fabric underneath for new clothes. Sewing for soldiers, especially for husbands or brothers, was a regular chore. Many women worked in clothing factories, producing the tens of thousands of uniforms needed by the army.

When the war ended in 1865, clothing shortages eased. Even so, most people tended clothing with care. Sunlight, moths, and the harsh washing methods of the day sometimes ruined clothes. One woman, fearful a favorite dress would shrink, wore it all summer long without washing it.

Women continued to recycle dresses. With the help of friends, relatives, and dressmakers, they turned the skirts of old dresses inside out to reuse the fabric. They restyled bodices and sleeves. One Illinois woman sewed a dress in 1865, then made the gown over four times. It was part of her wardrobe for over 30 years.

"JUST AS MUCH AS IN THE EAST"

The American frontier continued inching westward through the 1800s. Pioneers in western America knew their clothes often didn't meet the fashion standards of city dwellers back East. Their lives in mining camps, on sod-house farms and ranches required simple work clothes sewn from durable cloth. Buckskin had remained a staple of pioneer wardrobes for over 200 years.

A Civil War veteran returned to his not-so-fashionable western home.

Yet when the first years of hardship ended, westerners hoped for more up-to-date fashions. Women on remote homesteads devoured fashion magazines, even when the latest finery was impractical or not available. "Because I must wear calico," wrote one Kansas woman, "must I also be deprived of the pleasure of admiring the beautiful attire of my more fortunate sisters?"

Another Kansas woman defended western fashion. "People are generally . . . not half so heathenish as many imagine," she wrote to her local paper. "... People expect taste and tidiness in dress, at least in ladies, just as much as in the East." Taste and tidiness did not equal up-to-date fashion, however.

Fashions such as the huge hoop skirt did eventually travel west. A woman wrote from the California Trail in June 1857:

> There is a bride & groom in the Inman party. The bride wears hoops. We have read of hoops being worn, but they had not reached Kansas before we left so these are the first we've seen and would not recommend them for this mode of traveling. In asides the bride is called "Miss Hoopy."

A lasting original of American fashion was born in the gold-mining camps of California during the 1850s. Miners needed rugged clothes to survive rocks, mud, and water. A San Francisco tailor named Levi Strauss sewed some work pants out of a heavy-duty fabric he'd hoped to sell as tent canvas. Soon miners were asking for "those pants of Levi's." As demand skyrocketed, Strauss replaced the tent fabric with denim, dyed blue to hide stains—and blue jeans were born.

NATIVE AMERICAN CLOTHING

Western lands were home to many different Native American tribes. In many respects, Native American clothing, made of materials close at hand and styled on what the climate demanded, proved more practical than the outfits of white settlers.

In most tribes, women prepared their family's clothing. The Pueblo tribes made cloth from cotton plants. Some they traded to other tribes for animal skins, the most common material used for Indian clothing. The Apache made clothes from deerskin using sinews from the animal's back leg for thread. Spanish explorers had introduced sheep to the Indians of the Southwest in the 1500s; tribes such as the Navajo came to excel at weaving wool for clothes and blankets. In the Pacific Northwest, women wove beautiful fringed blanket shawls.

On the Great Plains, enormous herds of buffalo provided tribes with plentiful food and with warm skins for clothing. Tanning a buffalo hide took three to six days. Women stretched the skin on the ground, scraped off fat and tissue, treated the hide with chemicals made from the animal's brain, liver, and fat, then worked it into a soft material. Clothing made from hides—robes and dresses, leggings and moccasins—dripped with fringe. The finest clothes were bone white, showed no holes, and felt soft as a breeze.

Many tribes decorated their clothes with geometric designs and depictions of plants and animals. Often decorative elements were sacred

A Sioux boy in moccasins and leggings

Beads and fringe adorned this Apache woman's soft dress.

symbols: a feather signified protection, a color represented the power of the earth. Among the Lakota, a tribal leader was awarded a specially decorated shirt along with the title "shirt wearer."

Beads adorned the clothing of many tribes from the Great Lakes to the Great Plains. Beads were made from shells, stones, seeds, bones, and, later, glass supplied by white traders. Beading required skill and patience. An Ojibway bandolier bag (worn like a sash over one shoulder and across the chest and back) might take a woman one year to bead.

Native Americans also used dyed porcupine quills and bird quills for decoration. Quilling required the mastery of nine different skills. Cheyenne women who were expert in quilling belonged to an exclusive quilling society. Women also decorated clothing with paints, scalp locks, shiny bits of tin, and feathers.

By the late 1860s, white Americans had pushed westward and forced most native people to live on reservations. Because Indian men

Indian boys in white-styled clothes in the 1880s

were no longer allowed to hunt, women had no hides to tan. They had to turn instead to bolts of cheap fabric, handed out by the U.S. government. Most native people eventually had to abandon their traditional clothing and adopt white dress. When some Indian children were taken from their families and sent to boarding schools, they were not only forced to speak English, but also to dress in white-styled clothes. Government officials believed "civilized" clothing helped hide the children's "savage" heritage.

"IF I HAD NOT A MACHINE"

Sewing clothes remained painstaking work in the early 1800s. Thanks to the fabric-making machines developed in the late 1700s, women no longer had to make their own cloth; but they still toiled for hours, necks aching, eyes straining, and fingers stinging from pushing a needle through heavy fabrics.

Most women sewed their families' undergarments, shirts, aprons, and children's clothes, and at least part of their own wardrobe. Old clothes often served as patterns for cutting out new ones. Women helped one another with fittings. Few days passed when some sewing or mending was not done. A Wisconsin teacher's 1845 journal included these entries: "June 23, Monday: I have been fitting a dress for Phebe since school. . . . June 25, Wednesday: I fitted Jane a dress this noontime."

Then in 1846, Elias Howe changed the making of clothes forever by patenting a new invention, the sewing machine. Howe's machine, powered by a hand-turned crank, could sew five times faster than a person could sew by hand. Even so, a seamstress had to stop her cranking frequently as she sewed; her hands were needed to adjust the fabric and move it along. Howe's machine was quickly improved

Sewing machines made "Splendid presents!" according to one magazine in about 1870.

upon by Isaac Singer, who, in the 1850s, developed a machine powered by a foot treadle. Hands freed, a seamstress could easily keep the fabric moving beneath the needle.

The first sewing machines were most commonly used by professional dressmakers and tailors, who provided the skilled fitting necessary for a well-made garment. *Godey's Lady's Book* noted that an average family hired a dressmaker for about a week each spring and fall at a charge of 75¢ a day. A woman saved by having a dressmaker sew only a gown's bodice, then finishing the gown herself. "Some of our most fashionable ladies make their own dresses," *Godey's* encouraged readers in 1851.

Around 1870, a sewing machine cost $64—not cheap for most families. Yet most women rated sewing machines high on their wish lists. A shirt that had required 14 hours of work by hand needed less than an hour and a half of work with a sewing machine. Labor on a man's frock coat reduced from over 16 hours to less than 3. One woman, making shirts for her husband during the Civil War, noted how lucky she was. "If I had not a machine, I should feel that I had quite a job on my hands," she wrote, ". . . but I shall soon have them done."

In the late 1850s, the *New York Tribune* recognized the revolution spurred by the sewing machine. "The more work can be done, the cheaper it can be done by means of machines—the greater will be the demand," it prophesied. "People will . . . dress better, change oftener, and altogether grow better looking."

PATTERNS

Another innovation came in 1859 when a New England dressmaker promoting herself under the French-sounding name of "Madame Demorest" ended the guesswork of cutting out fabric by introducing the first paper patterns. Offering "Practical Utility, Artistic Accuracy, & Fashionable Elegance," Madame Demorest's patterns sold in the millions. In 1863 Ebenezer Butterick also began selling patterns; Britain's Queen Victoria was among his millions of customers. Some companies packaged patterns in kits that included uncut cloth, thread, and trimmings. The cheapest kit for a dress of cambric cost $1.10, while homemakers dished out $25.65 for a gown of silk or satin.

Patterns, as well as the sewing machine, allowed an American woman of any income to dress almost as well as any other. All incomes followed the same fashion trends. The differences in a poorer woman's dress showed in its inexpensive fabric and trims.

Hints from magazines also showed poorer women how to achieve the fashionable look wealthier women enjoyed. One of the cheapest ways to update an old dress, according to one magazine, was simply to sew on new sleeves. Hoop skirts measured as much as 15 feet around at the hem—quite an investment in fabric. *Peterson's* magazine advised women to save money by making just one skirt and wearing it alternately with two bodices, one "for ordinary wear, and one . . . for occasions when more formal dress is required."

READY-TO-WEAR

During the Civil War, as Northern factories filled the demand for tens of thousands of uniforms, they had begun recording soldiers' measurements to provide better-fitting garments. Thanks to these measurements, patterns for men's clothing became available in standardized sizes.

The sewing machine, patterns, and standardized sizes all spurred the manufacture of ready-to-wear. Much of a man's wardrobe, which was simpler than a woman's, was soon being sewn in factories. It became cheaper to buy a man's suit ready-made than to pay a tailor to make one, or even to sew it at home. In 1866 an entire factory-made suit—coat, vest, and trousers—could be purchased for $9.50. A winter overcoat cost $30.00.

By 1869, railroad lines crossed the nation, and mail-order catalogs soon followed. Anywhere trains stretched to distant villages, anywhere traveling peddlers and tiny shops supplied customers, anywhere catalogs reached by mail, ready-to-wear clothes for men could be found.

"Gents furnishings" could be found in any remote country store by century's end.

By the end of the century, almost all men's clothing was sold ready-made in catalogs or in stores.

In an era in which the facade of "proper" dress was so important, Americans could move up the social ladder with ease. "Every sober mechanic has his one or two suits of broadcloth," wrote editor Horace Greeley, "and, so far as mere clothes go, can make as good a display when he chooses, as what are called the upper classes." The popular Sears Roebuck catalog summed up the situation in an 1887 advertisement: "Goods suitable for the millionaire, at prices in reach of the millions."

EVOLUTION OF "SENSIBLE DRESS"

Compared with the previous generation who thought anything above an 18" waist clumsy, we are a race of Amazons.
— Janesville Weekly Gazette,
Janesville, Wisconsin,
January 16, 1895

A new silhouette in women's skirts was well in place by 1873. This time, fashion hoisted a skirt's fullness to the base of the spine. To exaggerate the new shape as much as possible, women strapped pads stuffed with horsehair to the back of their waists. Soon the pads enlarged into a cage called a bustle. Bustles dominated fashion through the 1880s. By 1885 even some small girls wore them. Inventors worked constantly to improve bustles. One "improvement" was an adjustable bustle, loaded with springs, so a woman could sit more comfortably.

Bustles restricted most activities for women; so did tight bodices, narrow sleeves, petticoats, and long trains that swept the ground. Designers piled on the decorations: swags, ruffles, cascades, and bows. A wife's elaborate clothes, and her inability to work in them, advertised

A woman's bustle dress. The girl's dress, **opposite,** *also displayed three tiers of skirts. The top tier probably gathered to a bow or bustle at the back.*

her husband's status and wealth. Even working women, however, followed the styles—tight bodices, bustles, and all. One woman complained that her servant girl created a bustle using feather dusters.

Accessories of the 1870s and 1880s included hair plumes, parasols, gloves, fans, and ornate jewelry of all sorts. Instead of bonnets, women wore small hats perched at an angle atop their hairdos. Ribbons, velvet flowers, and feathers adorned the hats.

Women continued wearing their hair long and pulled back from the face, usually piled atop the head. Ringlets created with a hot curling wand sometimes cascaded down the back. False curls were in demand; some women in hard times, like the character of Jo March in *Little Women,* cut and sold their hair to wig makers.

Society admired a woman's delicate nature, so women aimed for an "interesting pallor" instead of a rosy-cheeked look. With makeup frowned upon, women drank vinegar and ate chalk to achieve a pale complexion. They also nibbled wafers of arsenic. "An excellent medicine," promised one advertisement for arsenic, "for giving to the complexion a clearness and brilliancy not obtainable by external methods."

Boater hats and knickers, **left;** *man's suit of the 1870s,* **right.**

A woman who ate arsenic did indeed gain an increasingly pale, bluish tone, as the deadly poison affects the body's red blood cells.

THE MALE PERSPECTIVE

From the 1870s on, the frock coat shrank into a modern-looking jacket, cut short and square. Men wore their jackets buttoned high and opened low, showing off their vests and watch fobs. They oiled their short hair into place. Small-brimmed, rounded derby hats were popular.

Continuing the tradition of clean linen as the mark of a gentleman, businessmen preferred their shirts snowy white. In contrast, laborers often wore blue or gray shirts. Eventually, this difference distinguished "white-collar" and "blue-collar" work. Shirts now buttoned down the front instead of being pulled on over the head. Cuffs and collars, starched board stiff, were separate pieces that attached to a shirt.

A growing interest in sports influenced men's leisure clothes. Belted jackets, worn with knickers, were acceptable for golf, hunting, or cycling. Men donned boaters—straw sailor hats—and soft caps with visors. America's first professional baseball team, the Cincinnati Red Stockings, introduced baseball caps in 1869. The first rubber-and-canvas shoes appeared in 1868. By 1873, the shoes were called "sneakers" because of their quiet tread.

DRESS REFORM

In the mid-1800s, feminists and women's clubs had begun calling for an end to clothing that hampered comfort and movement. A tireless advocate for women's rights, Elizabeth Cady Stanton, believed a woman's "tight waist and long trailing skirts deprive her of all freedom." Amelia Bloomer, editor of a magazine supporting women's rights, complained that "woman has always sacrificed her comfort to fashions."

Bloomer began to wear dresses made like other fashionable dresses, but with one shocking difference. The skirts were knee length. A proper woman did not reveal her legs, however. Even when swimming, women and girls covered up with long wool trousers beneath bathing dresses. To cover her legs, Bloomer wore baggy Turkish trousers, gathered at the ankle, under her dress. When Bloomer described the costume in her magazine, the *Lily,* newspapers picked up the story and dubbed the trousers "bloomers."

Some women gratefully adopted bloomers. One Kansas pioneer found bloomers "well suited to a wild life like mine. Can bound over the prairies like an antelope, and am not in so much danger of setting my clothes on fire while cooking . . . I would not submit myself to wearing long dresses, when I can go so nimbly around."

Physicians and health reformers saw the health advantages in freer clothes. As early as 1858, *Godey's* introduced "gymnastics" costumes for women, which were similar to bloomers. Students at women's colleges began to wear gymnastics costumes in physical education classes.

Dress reform had loud opponents, however. Most people viewed the bloomer costume with shock. Did women in trousers mean to abandon their homes and compete in the outside world with men? Much of 19th-century society—women and men—found this prospect frightening. Cartoons portrayed women in bloomers loitering on street corners smoking cigars.

Even *Godey's,* which had introduced women's gymnastics costumes, complained that wearing athletic clothes outside the gym was going too far. "Are we to be so athleticized," asked an article, "that we will disdain all fripperies and wear the garments once considered as the prerogative of our husbands and brothers?" *Godey's* declared, "Bloomers are too great a sacrifice for our sex ever to make, and . . . in skirts only can they maintain . . . in the eyes of men their womanliness."

Many women agreed. Despite reform efforts, most women clung to their long skirts even for active sports such as tennis, hiking, and horseback riding. Many feminists abandoned bloomers, fearing the criticism would hurt their efforts to win voting and property rights for women.

Then, in the 1890s, a bicycle craze swept the country. Women joined wholeheartedly in the enthusiasm for the new sport, but found

These bloomer costumes were labeled, left to right: *"The Plain Dress," "Lady of Fashion," "Partial Reform," and "The Extreme Inovation [sic]."*

Women played sports in long skirts and corsets.

Culottes and a jacket with leg-of-mutton sleeves, about 1896

cycling in long skirts impossible. Thanks to the bicycle, some women finally began wearing bloomerlike outfits or shorter split skirts, called culottes, even at the price of hisses and boos.

GIBSON GIRLS

By the 1890s, women worked as teachers, as sales clerks, and as operators of two new inventions, the typewriter and the telephone. In 1893, *Harper's Weekly* praised the "evolution of sensible dress," saying it "had kept pace with women's expanded participation in colleges, in the professions and in the work force." "Sensible dress" meant the shirtwaist, a tailored, high-necked blouse. Worn with a flared skirt and sometimes a jacket, the shirtwaist contributed to a professional look—a version of a suit for women.

As the shirtwaist craze swept the country, a fresh new American ideal appeared. The "Gibson Girl," a creation of illustrator Charles Dana Gibson, personified the new look. Gibson's drawings portrayed a slim, athletic young woman, often in an outdoor setting, looking confident and healthy in shirtwaist and skirt. Her hair, swept back and up in a soft mound, was topped by an unadorned boater. Of course, women still required corsets and petticoats to achieve the "Gibson Girl" look, but gone at least were bustles and hoops. The overall effect was one of liberation—at least for the viewer of the clothes, if not for the woman wearing them.

Though easily sewn at home, the shirtwaist became the first garment for women to be mass-produced. Catalogs carried many pages of shirtwaist styles. *Vogue* informed readers in 1894, "Shirtwaists are

The Gibson Girl in boater, shirtwaist, and flared skirt

to be worn very much again this summer. . . .There are plenty of ready-made ones in all the shops that look very well indeed." By 1900, New York City had 462 busy shirtwaist factories.

TURN-OF-THE-CENTURY STYLE

Sleeves and skirts changed a woman's silhouette several times at the turn of the century. Huge leg-of-mutton sleeves, similar to those of the 1830s, were one short-lived fad. By 1900, a woman had normal shoulders again. Her silhouette was a pronounced S-curve, achieved with corsets that thrust her chest forward and arched her hips back— a look that was especially flattering to the mature woman.

To Americans, French fashion still symbolized wealth and refinement. America's new breed of wealthy families, rich from money made in railroads, mines, banks, and huge department stores, sailed straight to Paris for their wardrobes. Parisian fashion houses such as Charles F. Worth's dressed the wives of America's elite: the Vanderbilts, the Astors, and the Goulds. Some Paris designers opened showrooms in American cities.

Leg-of-mutton sleeves and plumes at the turn of the century

Left, *an actress wore the S-curve with melodramatic flare in 1902;* **right,** *the same silhouette on the wealthy Mrs. George Gould.*

At the end of the century and into the next, fashionable women wore huge hats piled with ribbon, velvet flowers, and plumes. Hats and hair had sported plumes for centuries; now entire stuffed birds sometimes nested on women's heads. The plume fad was killing five million birds per year, pushing some species to the brink of extinction. In 1896 a Boston group founded the Massachusetts Audubon Society to voice concerns over "a barbarous fashion." By 1913, state and federal laws prohibited the plume trade.

Children in sailor suits in the 1890s. The child at left is a boy. The older boy wears knickers with his coat.

CHILDREN'S DRESS

Like their mothers, girls abandoned bustles by the 1890s. Shirtwaists with large sleeves and collars, worn with shortened skirts, allowed them some freedom of movement. Girls still donned pinafores to protect their dresses. For play, some girls were allowed to wear culottes. Little boys continued in long curls and loose dresses.

In the late 1890s, America began building a "new navy" of modern, steam-powered ships. Patriotic enthusiasm for this endeavor led to the enormous popularity of sailor suits for both boys and girls.

Fashioned in shades of red, white, and blue, sailor suits sported middy collars and braid trim. In winter, children wore pea-coats like those worn by sailors. Black leather high-top shoes, laced or buttoned above the ankles, finished the costume.

Clothes were expensive, and children had to be careful of them. Soiled clothing had to be scrubbed by hand in a washtub and cranked through a wringer. A child who damaged his good clothes earned a scolding. Poorer children often dressed in hand-me-downs and went barefoot.

As in every generation, many children of this era yearned to dress in the latest fashions. A Wisconsin girl felt herself well dressed until viewing a group of girls in Chicago turned out all in white in the newest styles. "I felt I would like to hide myself," she wrote. A young lady whose mother disagreed with her about the style of a new dress recalled, "I wanted the shoulders out like all the other girls."

"THIS CLASS OF FACTORIES"

Demand for cloth and for ready-made clothing continued to grow as America's population grew. Throughout the 1800s, textile mill workers had fought for better working conditions, often by striking. They won some reforms such as the 10-hour workday. That progress eroded, however, as mills pulled more and more workers from the millions of poor people flooding in from Europe, hoping to find jobs and a better life in America. Many immigrants were Jews escaping from eastern Europe, desperate for work under any conditions. Differences in language and customs among groups of immigrants hampered their ability to organize against mill owners. Consequently, working conditions worsened.

By the late 1890s, several hundred thousand people worked in textile mills. They labored from 12 to 17 hours a day. They went deaf from noisy machines. They grew ill from breathing machinery fumes and lint particles. Some died after only a few years in these conditions. Many workers were only children.

Thousands of people cut and sewed in clothing factories, soon labeled "sweatshops." From dawn to dark, workers crammed into dirty, poorly ventilated rooms where diseases such as tuberculosis spread easily. One New York City inspector complained in 1887:

> The buildings are ill smelling from cellar to garret. The people are huddled together too closely for comfort. . . . It seems wonderful that there exists a human being that could stand it for a month and live. We are not describing one or two places, for there is hardly an exception in this class of factories in all New York.

Whole families also did factory-type work at their homes, sewing for pennies per garment. Often they sewed "sections," repeating the same job—hemming, sewing buttonholes, fitting sleeves—on garment after garment. These workers barely earned enough to survive, yet

Girls in a textile mill, about 1910

they sometimes had to buy their own needles, scissors, and other supplies, and to pay for any work ruined.

In 1900 the International Ladies Garment Workers Union and the Amalgamated Clothing Workers of America formed to fight for better wages and working conditions. Over the following years, workers repeatedly struck for fewer hours, more pay, and an end to child labor. Then, on March 25, 1911, a fire broke out at the Triangle shirtwaist factory in New York City. Young female workers had been locked in by factory owners to keep the girls from leaving. There was only one fire escape, and it collapsed. Many young women leapt from upper-story windows. "It was jump or be burned," recalled a witness. ". . . A heap of corpses lay on the sidewalk." Firemen found 50 bodies piled behind the locked doors. In all, 146 girls died.

In December an all-male jury acquitted the factory owners of any responsibility. One juror blamed the victims, noting, "I think that the girls, who undoubtedly have not as much intelligence as others might have in other walks of life, were inclined to fly into a panic."

The following year, 20,000 workers walked out at a Lawrence, Massachusetts, textile mill when owners cut wages. At one point during the strike, police beat a group of 150 striking women and children. Public outcry forced a congressional investigation. Eventually, the workers regained their lost wages as well as other benefits. The Lawrence strike, coupled with the Triangle tragedy, raised awareness in the public and government of the terrible conditions in the garment industry.

CLOTHES IN HARD TIMES

A flare of footlights, . . . the curtains part, and America passes judgment on what America can do.

—Vogue, 1914, heralding the first American fashion show

As the 20th century opened, women's fashion continued to flirt with styles. Some dresses flowed. "Hobble" skirts narrowed so much that they hobbled the wearer into mincing baby steps three inches long. Women continued wearing huge hats. By 1915, skirts shortened to the ankle.

A revolution in shrinking underwear was underway. In 1916 the first brassieres, or bras, arrived from France. Girdles made from a new rubber material were lighter than corsets, yet still squeezed women into the desired shape. For babies, leak-proof rubber pants, worn over diapers, arrived. For the first time, toddler-age boys could wear trousers instead of dresses.

SHOPPING

About 60 percent of America's population still lived on farms. The U.S. postal service added rural delivery in 1902 and parcel post in 1913, and catalog sales boomed. Rural folks could stay as up-to-date

Narrow skirts and full hats, about 1911. Buckled shoes echoed those of the 1700s.

as city dwellers. New roads and railroad lines helped speed orders to customers.

Department stores stocked modestly priced copies of high fashion from Paris. Magazines warned women that claims of an authentic Parisian label were probably "fraudulent." To entice female customers, department stores such as Macy's in New York City and Marshall Field in Chicago hired women salesclerks. Stores also added tearooms, lunch counters, and "ladies waiting rooms" so women could shop the whole day long.

ERA OF CHANGE

The United States entered World War I (1914–1918) in June 1917. For the first time, women joined the American armed services. About 12,500 women in the U.S. Marine Corps were called "marinettes." Women's uniforms, olive and khaki like men's, included skirts. Civilian women performed a wide variety of wartime jobs. Most worked

Woman at work during World War I

***Edward Windsor and the
Windsor knot***

in ankle-length dresses. Some, especially in factories and on farms, opted to wear trousers.

By the time the armistice was declared on November 11, 1918, the U.S. had lost 112,000 soldiers. The war's dreadful slaughter staggered people. The sight of so many women in black crepe was unbearable, and strict mourning etiquette began to crumble. By 1920, women wore mourning for just a year. Crepe sales dropped and never recovered.

Men's clothing aimed for comfort after the war. Dress shirts softened. Sweaters were seen everywhere, especially paired with knickers on the golf course. Shoes that tied replaced shoes that buttoned.

The most influential man of fashion for several decades was the heir to the British throne, Edward Windsor, Prince of Wales. "The average young man in America," noted *Men's Wear* magazine, "is more interested in the clothes of the Prince of Wales than in the clothes of any other individual on earth." Following Edward's lead, men adopted loose trousers and jackets with fitted waists. Ties sported "Windsor" knots.

Fashion for women again appeared in turmoil. Should women abandon pants and return to prewar styles? Wearing the "pants in the family" meant being in charge. With husbands and fathers back home, women in pants returned to dresses. But change was in the air. In August 1920, after decades of lost battles, American women won the right to vote through the 19th Amendment to the U.S. Constitution. Women's new freedom at the ballot box soon mirrored a new freedom in clothes.

THE ROARING '20S

A restless yet confident spirit invigorated America in the 1920s. The new decade transformed young women's fashion as never before. For the first time, women grabbed their long hair, which had always been so time-consuming to style, and snipped it off. "Bobbed" hair was all the rage. The boyish bob was chin length or even shorter. A sleek cut that swung close to the face, the bob called for a hat that also hugged the head. Women donned bell-shaped *cloche* hats (French for "bell") that defied the wind better than the old-fashioned, wide-brimmed hats when taking a spin in the new automobiles.

Popular silent screen star Clara Bow symbolized the new woman of the boisterous Roaring '20s. One beauty shop operator set a chair outside a movie theater and advertised, "Enjoy the Clara Bow haircut then be our guest to enjoy Clara Bow in *Love among the Millionaires.*" The sparkling new woman was christened a "flapper," a British term for a fledgling young lady. The flapper exhibited her freedom by danc-

Flappers' short skirts and bold ways shocked people.

Laced boots, silk stockings, and tank suits were 1920s beachwear.

ing to jazz, smoking cigarettes, and driving cars. She painted on lipstick and rouge produced by cosmetics companies run by women such as Helena Rubinstein and Elizabeth Arden.

Rejecting corsetted "wasp" waists, women instead wore dresses that had no waistline at all. Although women hid their curves in the tubular silhouette, they revealed more skin. All through the decade, skirts inched higher and higher. Some states considered fines for dresses shorter than three inches above the ankle. But the trend was irreversible; by 1926, women's dresses rose, for the first time, *above* the knee. In place of heavy, dark stockings, women showed off their legs in sheer silk, or in hose made from the new "artificial silk," rayon. High-buttoned boots vanished, replaced by narrow, high-heeled shoes with flirty straps. Bathing costumes shrank to sleeveless tank suits.

A new French designer, Gabrielle "Coco" Chanel, called for simplicity in clothes. "Each frill discarded," she claimed, "makes one look younger." Chanel popularized sweaters, sailor pants, and short evening dresses. Her "little black dress" defined the tubular silhouette as one of elegant restraint. But even Chanel did not discard all frills; it was she who first popularized costume jewelry.

AN END TO GOOD TIMES

The roaring '20s screeched to a halt on October 21, 1929, when the U.S. stock market crashed, plunging the nation into economic chaos. By the end of the month, investors had lost $16 billion. Banks and factories closed; 14 million people lost their jobs. Thousands lined up for handouts of bread and soup. The country had entered the Great Depression.

To match the times, more somber, conservative clothes replaced the high-flying fashions of the 1920s. For both men and women, clothing colors darkened. Shoulder pads endowed clothes with a solid, square look that seemed to meet the depression's challenges head on. Men in "responsible positions are forced to dress in a conventional and conservative manner," noted a fashion book in 1937, "and consider it a virtue and a sign of position to do so."

For women, the tubular silhouette of the 1920s vanished. Waists reappeared. Skirts became narrow in the hips; women zipped into them with the help of girdles, now made of stretchy elastic. As if reflecting the country's spirits, hemlines fell, to about eight inches above the ground. A woman who could not afford new dresses sewed bands of fabric to her old clothes to achieve the longer hemline.

Above, *an old flapper-style coat over a newer dress with the longer hemline of the Great Depression.* **Left,** *actress Jean Harlow.*

Skirts and blouses, offered as "separates," extended a wardrobe for less money. Hair grew longer, subdued on the back of the neck in soft waves.

SILVER SCREEN GLAMOUR

To ease the sting of economic burdens, Americans looked to Hollywood. More than 85 million people a week escaped their troubles in darkened movie theaters. Many fans imitated the polished makeup of film stars: plucked eyebrows, dark lipstick, gleaming fingernails. Jean Harlow's blonde hair inspired millions to bleach their tresses. "Not that I expect to be rich, beautiful and courted like the stars of the screen," wrote one movie fan, "but because of my admiration for these lovely ladies, I keep myself better groomed; I watch my carriage [posture] and my complexion."

Movie star Clark Gable prompted thousands of male fans to go barechested in the 1930s.

As much as possible, women also emulated the clothing of the movie queens. In 1932, when Joan Crawford wore a frilly gown with wide shoulders, Macy's department store sold nearly half a million similar dresses. Men also copied their idols. Clark Gable took off his shirt in one movie and revealed that he had no undershirt beneath. Since not wearing an undershirt was a fashion anyone could immediately afford, undershirt sales plummeted.

Hollywood popularized an image of fitness; it became fashionable to show off a well-toned body. For swimming, men abandoned tank suits that covered their chests and, for the first time, appeared at beaches bare-chested. Some women tossed out their long tennis dresses and copied tennis champ Alice Marble, who in 1933 dared to wear shorts at Wimbledon.

Hollywood also promoted the tan. For centuries women had prized a pale complexion as a symbol of leisure. People who got tan worked outdoors doing manual labor. Now a tan advertised the leisure for

During the depression, young men at work took off their undershirts to get a Hollywood tan rather than the farmer version.

luxurious hours of tennis or swimming. Sunglasses became a popular new accessory.

The worst of the depression ended by 1936. Some Americans even found time and money for dressy gatherings. Like the new skyscrapers and art deco design, dressy clothes appeared streamlined. Women wore floor-sweeping evening gowns with a 1930s twist—plunging bare backs. The form-fitting gowns were made of silk, rayon, satin, and chiffon; actresses appeared at film premieres in shimmering lamé, a man-made fabric. Men looked dapper in tuxedos or dinner jackets. Perhaps couples hoped their clothes lent them the elegance of movie dancers Fred Astaire and Ginger Rogers.

Improvements in transportation and in clothing manufacture, such as factory assembly lines, filled department stores with fashionable clothing most people could afford. Science continued developing new

A form-fitting gown echoed art deco design.

In the late 1930s and early 1940s, women wore hats, mannish suits, and nylons with a seam down the back. Little girls' fashions echoed those of Shirley Temple.

textiles. In May 1940, women lined up for blocks to buy the first stockings made from nylon. This wonder fiber held its shape, breathed, and shed dirt better than silk; but it was just as silky sheer.

"MAKE IT DO OR DO WITHOUT"

The United States entered World War II (1939–1946) after the December 7, 1941, bombing of U.S. Navy ships at Pearl Harbor in Hawaii. Like other nations, the U.S. funneled every resource into an all-out war effort. Factories that had made consumer goods were suddenly producing planes, tanks, and uniforms. Media campaigns encouraged patriotic citizens to curb consumption for the duration of the war: "Use it up, wear it out, make it do or do without."

Since leather was needed for millions of pairs of combat boots, quantities of civilian shoes were limited. The American War Production Board issued ration coupons allowing each civilian three pairs of new shoes a year. Nylon was needed for parachutes, so women did without stockings. Some applied leg makeup to get the look of stockings. Many, especially those on farms or in factories, turned again to trousers and overalls. Metal used in zippers was also a valuable wartime commodity, so new dresses were zipperless. Japan had cut off much of America's rubber supply; any available rubber went into tires for military vehicles, not into women's girdles. Advertisers praised the "duration suit" with its adjustable waist, "designed for war with or without a girdle."

Fabric for uniforms for America's 16 million military men and women was a necessity. From 1942 to 1946 the American War Production Board issued regulations aimed at reducing fabric use among civilians by 15 percent. No fabric-on-fabric was allowed; pleats, pockets, ruffles, trouser cuffs, and wide lapels were out. Skirts, shortened to the knee, had hems no more than two inches deep.

Even swimsuit midriffs vanished. Noted the *Wall Street Journal,* "The two piece bathing suit now is tied in with the war as closely as the zipperless dress and the pleatless skirt." Three years later one designer introduced an especially tiny two-piece suit. He named it after a U.S. military site in the South Pacific, Bikini Atoll.

Women working in factories pinned their hair back to keep it safely out of machinery. Hairpins were scarce, so hair nets and scarves became wartime fashion. So did hairstyles such as the "Victory Roll" and the "Liberty Cut," which required few hairpins. Women needed ration coupons to buy hats, so older hats—or no hats at all—had to do.

TROUBLE AT HOME

Not everyone skimped on fabric during the war. Some young people, especially youths in urban areas such as Harlem and Los Angeles, favored a fashion called the zoot suit. The outfit featured an oversize jacket and trousers with deep pleats. A wide-brimmed hat, pointed shoes, and long greased hair, combed back off the face, completed the zoot-suit look.

"Zoot-suiters" angered some people, who believed the zoot suit flaunted wartime restrictions. The anger became racial, since many zoot-suiters were black or Hispanic youths. One political commentator felt the zoot suit was a means "to compensate for the sense of being neglected by society. The wearers are almost invariably the victims of poverty . . . and segregation." In June of 1943, a group of white

Style meant Zoot suits to these young men.

servicemen stationed near Los Angeles had a different opinion. They attacked a group of Mexican-American zoot-suiters, ripping off their clothes and cutting their hair. The incident sparked a riot that raged for two days.

AMERICA OR FRANCE?

Many French fashion houses closed down during the war. Those Paris designers still working seemed to be in league with the Nazis. The American War Production Board proposed censoring fashion news from France showing clothes that "are in flagrant violation of our imposed wartime silhouette."

American designers stepped into the vacuum. Working with fabrics not strictly rationed, such as denim and calico, they tried to make

"Victory Roll" hairstyles and the "Victory" sign went hand in hand for patriotic steel workers during World War II.

Two WWII veterans returning to their family in 1947 chose T-shirts as outer garments.

utilitarian clothes look fashionable. Claire McCardell led the way for sportswear for women. She popularized flat women's shoes when she asked Capezio to make a black ballet slipper with outdoor soles. Norman Norell offered sophisticated sheath dresses. *Harper's Bazaar* hailed the homegrown innovations: "We have learned from the greatest masters of fashion in the world. Learned, then added something of our own."

When the war ended, fashions worn on the battlefield, such as duffle coats and cotton T-shirts, came home to stay along with millions of soldiers. People were weary of scrimping on fabric, and men celebrated with double-breasted jackets and wider pants with cuffs. Women were eager for luxury. It came from a French designer, and, in one swoop, Paris regained fashion leadership.

DO YOUR OWN THING

We are searching for something. Clothes can change, women want to change.
> —American designer Norman Norell, 1966

Amidst a whirlwind of attention, French designer Christian Dior unveiled his "New Look" in 1947. American women adored it. The New Look dress featured a tiny wasp waist reminiscent of earlier times. Its billowing skirt measured as much as 15 feet around at the hem—a revival of 1850s fashion. Legs nearly disappeared beneath skirts that reached almost to the ankle.

For many, Dior's New Look represented a romantic softness after the boxy clothes of the war years. But beneath that soft illusion lurked a dress so stiff and full it could practically stand by itself. Once again women reshaped their bodies to fit a style, hooking on corsets, padding their bras, and donning stiff petticoats.

Critics claimed the New Look put women back "in their places." Some women picketed stores carrying Dior's collection. When Dior checked into a hotel in Chicago, protesters brought signs urging, "Women! Join the fight for freedom in manner of dress," and, "Mr. Dior, we abhor, dresses to the floor."

As always, however, fashion would not be denied. "The short skirt is out of the running," *McCall's* informed readers. "Even before governmental restrictions were taken off skirts, smart girls were letting hems down." Skirts that swooped low, said *McCall's*, were "the best looking clothes seen walking around New York."

A bride, **opposite,** *glowed in the New Look; her groom sported a flat-top haircut. The New Look drew approval throughout the 1950s,* **above.**

Wholesome teenagers rocked in the early 1950s.

"DUNGAREE DOLLS"

In the late 1940s, Americans discovered a new fashion consumer right in their own living rooms: the teenager. For centuries, society had dismissed youths as unfinished people rehearsing for adult life in copies of their parents' clothes. Suddenly, that view changed. Nearly half of the people in America were under age 25, and they had money to spend. Companies rushed to create products for this new-found market.

Teen fashion evolved in several directions during the 1950s. Holly-wood played a defining role. One wholesome image, wrapped up in actors such as Doris Day and Pat Boone, was the "girl and boy next door." Well-behaved girls dressed in long slim skirts or in full skirts over nylon net petticoats. A fitted blouse or twin sweater set, along with ankle socks and loafers or saddle shoes, completed the outfit. The hit songs "White Sports Coat" and "Blue Suede Shoes" reflected the clean-cut look of boys in sweaters, pressed slacks, and loafers or buckskin lace shoes.

Rebellious youths mimicked the new rock 'n' roll sensation, Elvis Presley, or actors Marlon Brando and James Dean. In the films *The Wild One* (1953) and *Rebel without a Cause* (1955), leather jackets and crumpled T-shirts symbolized a defiant disregard for rules. Rebels usually wore longer hair greased back off their faces.

Most teenagers, "greasers" or not, wore blue jeans, called dungarees. Another hit song, "Dungaree Doll," referred to a fad for girls—wearing a man's shirt untucked over jeans. Jeans were so central to America's fashion identity that they were displayed in the American exhibit at the 1958 World's Fair.

In the late 1950s, growing conflicts, including the cold war's nuclear threat and racial discrimination in America, led to the Where go? What do? What for? slogan of the beat generation. Beatniks gathered in coffee bars and jazz clubs to read poetry, listen to music, and hold intellectual discussions. They dressed in rumpled black clothes

Elvis Presley and the greaser look

that expressed their antiestablishment, antifashion attitude. Beat men wore turtlenecks or polo shirts, jeans or khakis. Women wore black skirts and tights, or calf-length pants called pedal pushers or Capris. Leotards, big sweaters called sloppy joes, and flat ballet-style shoes finished their look.

"BETTER THINGS FOR BETTER LIVING"

During the prosperous 1950s, advances in science and technology—the invention of computers, satellites, plastics, and new uses for chemicals—led Americans to expect a better life. By 1954, one-seventh of the population owned a television set. That number soon soared. New appliances, often in pastel shades, supposedly made women's lives "brighter—your daily chores lighter." To simplify the wave of buying, Americans began carrying plastic credit cards in their wallets.

Clothes had never been easier to keep clean. Instead of sudsing clothes in a washtub, a person could simply load an automatic washer. Ads urged women to "Throw Away Those Clothespins!" and

Appliances made Mom's life brighter.

use an automatic dryer as well. Even detergents improved, as chemists created soaps that did a better job of breaking down grease and dirt. Because clothes were easily washed, people added more pastel colors to their wardrobes.

Chemical companies such as DuPont created more easy-care fabrics. Orlon and dacron joined nylon in promising durability, quick drying, dirt and moth resistance, and less shrinking and ironing. Even crisp pleats held their shape when washed. The new fibers reduced the weight of clothes, especially in men's suits. Clothing made from these manmade fabrics, such as windbreakers, sold like crazy.

WHAT MOM AND DAD WORE

Women often wore sportswear such as slacks and sweaters; Claire McCardell, the leading designer of sportswear, even appeared on the cover of *Time* magazine in 1955. But the strongest image of women conveyed by the media was that of the perfect homemaker. Mom was portrayed working in full-skirted dresses, frilly aprons, and pointy-toed high heels.

In reality, many women worked outside the home in the 1950s. Businesswomen dressed in feminine, close-fitting suits and the same pointy-toed heels. Dior's wasp waist still reigned in both everyday dress and strapless long gowns. By the late 1950s, skirts shortened once again to the knee.

Men's appearance mirrored the nation's growing prosperity. Their short hair and clean-shaven faces reflected dependability. The gray flannel suit, worn with a white shirt and dark tie, became the business uniform. Dad relaxed on winter weekends in loose trousers and cardigan sweaters. In summer, he chose Bermuda shorts and colorful Hawaiian shirts.

In the early 1960s, America's First Lady, Jacqueline Kennedy, became a fashion trendsetter. "Jackie" dressed in suits, skinny pants, and evening gowns created by famous designers. During her first 16 months in the White House, Mrs. Kennedy reportedly spent $50,000 on clothes. Women copied her sophisticated, yet often simple, styles, down to her pillbox hat and bouffant hair. "When Jacqueline Kennedy accepts [fashions]," reported *Redbook* magazine, "the public sees the green light."

MODERN COOL

Rock 'n' roll, blues, and soul contributed to youth fashion throughout the 1960s. African-American musicians introduced huge "Afro" cuts for hair. Elements from the Orient, Africa, the Middle East, and the Caribbean crept into jewelry and clothes.

Motown singers were recognized for their slick, sophisticated looks. Male groups such as the Four Tops performed in colorful matching suits, while a popular female threesome, the Supremes, glittered in glamorous gowns and bouffant hairdos. The cropped hairstyle of the Beatles, the most influential band of the decade, was widely followed in America and Europe.

At the same time, the American space program was also influencing modern cool. On July 24, 1969, nearly 600 million people

The Supremes glittered in op-art gowns and bouffant hair.

around the world watched the seemingly impossible on television: Neil Armstrong made the first dusty footprint on the moon.

Fashion reflected the times in "mod" clothes made from sleek vinyl, plastics, even paper. Op art, a decorative style featuring geometric shapes and lines, popped on fabrics in bold primary colors and dramatic black and white. Hair also looked geometric, worn short and sculpted or long and straight. Women gooped their eyes with black eyeliner and colored eye shadow. Lips disappeared, painted pale, whitish colors. The Beatles took on the mod look, too, moving from narrow dark suits to zippered ankle boots and collarless jackets.

Many Americans tuned their televisions to *Star Trek* and saw a 1960s version of what clothes would be like in the 23rd century,

The Beatles in one of many looks they chose over the years—cropped hair and collarless jackets.

A chain belt gave a miniskirt a mod look.

complete with very short skirts for women. In real life, the biggest trend in women's fashion was the miniskirt. Introduced in London boutiques by designer Mary Quant and others, the mini had a hemline eight or nine inches above the knee, exposing more skin than any previous skirt. "The young recognize no boundaries and feel no . . . commitments," proclaimed a *New York Times Magazine* article. "Short skirts, some say, are a sign." A sign of what? The mini certainly seemed a sign of freedom in women's clothes.

But how were women supposed to sit or bend without exposing more than they wished? Patterned tights and the first panty hose resolved that problem, but not another. Skimpy minis looked best on slim young women such as supermodel Twiggy, who stood 5 feet 7 inches tall but weighed only 99 pounds. To help women look like Twiggy, Elizabeth Arden's New York salon offered exercises and massage for pudgy knees. Few, however, could achieve the lean, leggy look necessary for minis. Most older women avoided the short skirt rage. By the decade's end, the mini was joined by midi and maxi skirts, reaching to mid-calf and ankle.

"ALL YOU NEED IS LOVE"

A decidedly different look evolved in San Francisco in the late 1960s. A group of young adults called hippies shocked people with their carefree lifestyles, which included the use of drugs such as marijuana and LSD. With race riots tearing American cities apart and American television news showing young soldiers dying in Vietnam, hippies turned their backs on traditional Western values. "Make love, not war" became

Hippies preached "flower power."

a hippie theme. Hippies staged sit-ins and passed out flowers symbolizing peace. "Aggressively pushing their nonaggressive credo," noted *Newsweek* in 1967, hippies "are antagonizing the squares, frightening the authorities and driving the cops crazy."

The hippies' dress reflected their break with society. A canvas of self-expression, clothes bloomed with painted flowers, beading, and embroidery. Clouds of tie-dyed colors or psychedelic swirls of "acid colors"—orange, lime green, purple, and hot pink—floated on shirts. Both sexes wore jeans, sandals, and flowing caftans.

Young males grew their hair to shoulder length. They strutted like peacocks in exotic prints, ruffled shirts, and jewelry. Not since the

Long hair and decorated bell bottoms on a hippie man

1700s had men dressed so flamboyantly. "The once securely but-toned-down fortress of male fashion," noted *Newsweek* in 1968, "is clearly under siege." Meanwhile, young women wore jackets from the army surplus store. Older folks complained that they couldn't tell the boys from the girls. "Men's clothes have become an approximation of women's, and women's clothes copy men's," one psychologist noted. "When clothes express such confused roles—society is in trouble."

Hippie fashion soon became a norm among America's youth. American teenagers spent $3.5 billion a year to look "groovy." Jeans with holes and ragged hems became a new teen uniform. Hip-hugging pants made of materials from denim to velvet were accentu-ated by wide belts; bell-bottoms flared below the knee. For most teens, the hippie look had nothing to do with a hippie lifestyle, and it soon lost much of its protest significance.

WOMEN IN PANTS

As the 1970s opened, many women, burned out on skirts by the mini, began to wear pants. Pants sold so well that major designers added pantsuits—including some for elegant evening wear—to their collections. In 1968, Levi's launched a "division for gals." Some busi-nesses began to accept female employees in pants. One survey reported that Macy's department store would not permit women employees in pants, but the First National Bank of Boston would "if they continued to act like women." AT&T would keep "an open mind."

For the first time in America's fashion history, women began to have a real choice between dresses and pants. Mistress Fuller, or any woman of the 1600s or 1700s, never would have dreamed of pulling on a pair of breeches. For centuries, men's clothing had symbolized their ability to move freely in the world. Constricting fashions for women confined them more closely to home. "Woman . . . has all the desire to conquer worlds," reported a fashion magazine in 1858, "but no worlds to conquer . . . She . . . finds nothing to strive for but the attention of gentlemen." A little more than a century later, women were striving in many worlds, from the classroom, to the halls of Congress, to the cubicles of AT&T.

OUR FASHION LEGACY

Open a closet. Clothes for work, play, dress up, and sleep crowd the space. Pull out a drawer, and clothes for cold, warm, sunny, or rainy days are stacked in heaps. Drawers brimming with garments would have been unimaginable to a woman preparing her own cloth, or sewing most of her family's wardrobe. She never could have produced so much.

Americans today are bombarded with choices when selecting fashions. The pace at which styles change has accelerated with each new generation. No longer dependent on fashion dolls crossing the Atlantic on ships, fashion now heralds new styles every season. The occasional fad still entices people into bizarre and uncomfortable clothes, but most often, our choices match our own personal notion of comfort, function, and good style.

Few people stray too far from what society approves as proper attire. Sumptuary laws pinned people in their social places. Abigail Adams longed for a few "fripperies" to "look like the rest of the world." *Godey's Lady's Book* admonished readers to "conform." Then and now, teenagers beg to dress like their friends. Yet fashion also offers the chance for individual expression. From the flamboyant dress of the flappers, to bloomers, zoot suits, and hippie garb, clothes have long advertised personal identity.

What Americans wear changes, but people's love of fashion never does. Alice Roosevelt Longworth, daughter of President Theodore Roosevelt, lived a long and spirited life. In 1978, at age 94, she reflected on an old photograph of herself in a turn-of-the-century dress. Though the times, and the styles, had certainly changed, the long-lived Mrs. Longworth could still say, as she studied her young self, "Isn't this portrait pure rapture? What an incredible dress."

Alice Roosevelt Longworth's memorable dress of the early 1900s

SELECTED BIBLIOGRAPHY

Baker, Patricia. *The 1940s.* Fashions of a Decade Series. New York: Facts on File, 1992.

_____. *The 1950s.* Fashions of a Decade Series. New York: Facts on File, 1991.

Batterberry, Michael and Ariane. *Mirror, Mirror: A Social History of Fashion.* New York: Holt, Rinehart and Winston, 1977.

Bennett, Anna. *Fans in Fashion.* Vermont: Charles E. Tuttle Co., for the Fine Arts Museum of San Francisco, 1981.

Blum, Stella, editor. *Fashion and Costume from Godey's Lady's Book.* New York: Dover Publications, Inc., 1985.

_____. *Everyday Fashion of the Thirties as Pictured in Sears Catalog.* New York: Dover Publications, Inc., 1986.

Carter, Alison. *Underwear: The Fashion History.* New York: Drama Book Publishers, 1992.

Connikie, Yvonne. *The 1960s.* New York: Facts on File, 1990.

Costantino, Marie. *The 1930s.* New York: Facts on File, 1992.

Cotter, Ann, editor. *With Grace and Favor: Victorian and Edwardian Fashion in America.* Cincinnati: Cincinnati Art Museum, 1993.

Lester, Katherine, and Kerr, Rose. *Historic Costume.* Peoria, Illinois: Chas. A. Bennett Co., Inc., 1967.

Metropolitan Museum of Art. *The Eighteenth Century Woman.* New York: The Metropolitan Museum of Art, 1981.

Murray, Maggie. *Changing Styles in Fashion: Who, What, Why.* New York: Fairchild Publications, 1989.

Olian, JoAnne, editor. *Everyday Fashion 1909–1920 as Pictured in Sears Catalog.* New York: Dover Publications, Inc., 1995.

Schnurnberger, Lynn. *Let There Be Clothes.* New York: Workman Publishing, 1991.

Severa, Joan. *Dressed for the Photographer: Ordinary Americans and Fashion, 1840–1900.* Kent, Ohio: Kent State University Press, 1995.

Smithsonian Institution. *All Roads Are Good: Native Voices on Life and Culture.* Washington, DC: Smithsonian Institution Press, 1994.

Taylor, Lou. *Mourning Dress: A Costume and Social History.* London: George Allen and Unwin, 1983.

Time-Life Books. *All the Rage.* Alexandria, Virginia: Time-Life Books, 1992.

Weatherford, Dorris. *American Women's History.* New York: Prentice Hall, 1994.

Worrell, Estelle. *Children's Costume in America.* New York: Charles Scribner's Sons, 1980.

INDEX

ACKNOWLEDGMENTS

Photographs and illustrations used with permission of Brown Brothers: pp. 2, 9, 24, 33, 39, 44, 47, 49, 50 (left), 53 (bottom), 57 (right), 63, 67, 69 (top); Corbis: pp. 6, 11, 19, 48, 50 (right), 56; Corbis-Bettmann: pp. 10, 16, 27, 34, 43, 55, 62, 82; Archive Photos: pp. 13, 21, 28, 53 (top), 58, 66, 70, 85; IPS: p. 17; Colonial Williamsburg: p.18; Library of Congress: pp. 23, 26, 31, 37, 41, 57 (left), 71, 91, 92, 96; Tony Stone Images/Hulton Getty: pp. 25, 32, 54, 80; National Archives: pp. 36, 42; Museum of American Textile History: p. 60; UPI/Corbis-Bettmann: pp. 64, 72, 75, 76, 86, 87, 88; Hirz/Archive Photos: p. 65; Hollywood Book and Poster: pp. 69 (bottom), 81; collection of Ruth Giegerich: p. 73; collection of C. A. and Gwendolyn Christiansen: p. 77; collection of Paul and Joan Friant: p. 78; Daily Mirror/Corbis-Bettman: p. 79; Penguin/Corbis-Bettman: p. 84.

Front cover: Brown Brothers
Back cover: American Stock/Archive Photos

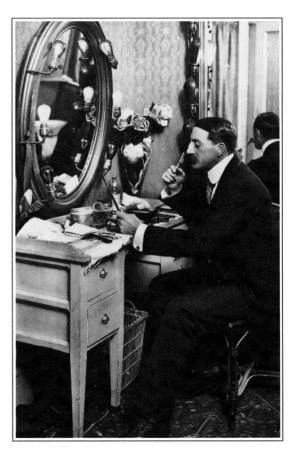

An actor combed his stylish mustache in 1902.

For more information about the award-winning People's History series, please call 1-800-328-4929 or visit www.lernerbooks.com